WORDS
TI
CAN

Katie B Morgan

Katie is a decorative painter, restorer and illustrator living in the
Cotswolds. It was in the last few years that she was fortunate to meet
Sonia Rolt. Sonia wished Katie well in putting this little book together.
Katie was first introduced to working boats and Gas Street basin,
Birmingham in the late 70's early eighties. ....the tail end... before the
canals were 'scrubbed up'. It was at this time that her love of wood
graining began when she was shown a set of combing tools by Ian Sly.
Her interest in words and folk art have led her to create a set of books,
all based on old trades and ways of life.

Sonia Rolt OBE
1919-2014
Sonia first worked on the canals during WW2. Her work led her to a
lifetime of conserving canals, industrial heritage and historic buildings.

Thanks to everyone on and by the cut who helped with words and meanings.

To Johnjo

WORDS
FROM THE CANAL

Katie B Morgan

Volume Two

Number one - *Owner boater.*

Coal box - *A box step down into cabin, often used for storing a bit of coal.*

Cut - *Canal or artificial channel.*

Winding hole - *A wider part of the canal that gives room for a narrowboat to turn.*

Valley - *Canal embankment.*

Bargee - *Skipper or owner of barge.*

Coaming - *Vertical edging around hatch, to keep water out.*

Draught - *Depth of boat beneath water. Vertical measurement between waterline and bottom of hull.*

Stern - *Back of boat, opposite of bow.*

Master -*Person in charge of boat.*

Mate- *Hired help.*

Windlass - *Metal handle used to crank lock paddles.*

To lock - *To work a boat through a lock.*

Draw - *To allow water to escape.*

Lower, drop or shut in - *Opposite of draw.*

Pots - *Socket at the bottom of a lock.*

Gudgen / tan pin - *A pin at the heel of a lock gate.*

Back flush - *A wave of water rebounding off lock gates when going downhill.*

Dandy paddle - *Top paddle.*

Flight - *Series of locks going uphill with a pound between them.*

Staircase locks / risers - *A series of locks without a pound between them.*

Button fender - *Cylinder shape, rope fender fixed by chains to stem or stern of narrowboat.*

Tipcat - *Curved banana shaped rope fenders on stern of narrow boats.*

Cross straps - *Two short ropes used to haul an empty boat away from a motor boats studs.*

Downhill runner - *A rope used for checking boats when going down in a lock.*

Snatcher - *A short tow rope.*

Strings - *Thin ropes used for tying planks or cloths.*

Turk's Head - *Decorative knot work.*

Snubber - *A thick rope used for towing.*

Warp - *Rope part of cable attached to anchor.*

Scend - *Space between the boats bottom and the waterways bed.*

Keb - *Tool used to drag coal out of the cut.*

Boat-hook - *Approximately an 8ft wooden pole with a metal point and hook on the end. Good for cleaning up blades.*

Sacrificial node - *Large pieces of metal, (usually magnesium) fixed under the waterline on the hull and allowed to corrode.*

Air draught - *Overall height of boat from water line up.*

Bilge - *Line along hull sides where the side and bottom meet.*

Ring-hole deep - *Overladen boat.*

Superstructure - *Structure of boat above the gunwale level.*

Butty - *Boat without an engine. Often has a large decorated tiller arm and bigger boatman's cabin.*

Rams head - *A butty's wooden rudder post.*

Helum / Elum - *Rudder and tiller combined.*

Ippey Cut - *The Wilts and Berks Canal.*

Loose by - *To let another boat overtake.*

Jam Hole - *Kearley and Tonge's jam factory at Southall.*

Stem - *Using the bow to push against, such as the bank when winding.*

Pair - *Two boats working together, one without an engine.*

Thick - *A line of locks that are close together.*

Freshet - *Rain causing increase in river flow.*

Queaches - *Wet muddy areas near canal*

When the canals were first built, families stayed in houses in the local towns but in the 1840's families began to live on the boats. The new railways had made it cheaper to transport goods so wages for the boaters had gone down. The lack of money to pay rents, meant that the wives and children move onto the boats. They all worked on the boats but it was only the captain that got paid. The Canal Boats Act in 1877 tried to improve conditions by limiting the cabins to be home for two adults and two children under twelve, and to shorten the working day. 1844 Inspectors checked on the size of families working on boats and tried to encourage children to go to school.

Flag - *An apron.*

Joey - *An odd-job person.*

Raff merchant - *Marine store dealer.*

Fly boats - *Boats that worked night and day and had priority at locks and bridges, usually worked by a team of men in shifts. The original horse drawn fly boats had used at least two horses for speed, often cantering.*

Northwich - *Boat built for the Grand Union C.C.C, by Yarwoods Ltd in Northwich Cheshire.*

Swans neck - *Shaped steel bar connecting the top of rudder to the tiller.*

Tiller - *Decorative and often removable bar on top of Swan's neck.*

Fly rink - *A term for a polished bald head in 1870's.*

Stroudwater barges - *Boats working on canal around Stroud, Gloucestershire.*

Dumb lighter - *Flat bottomed barge for carrying heavy loads, needing to be towed or pushed*

Quant - *Norfolk name for pole or shaft.*

Shaft - *Pole*

To shaft - *Alternative to legging.*

Spread, sprit - *Fenland term for shaft.*

Stemmed up - *Running aground.*

Punt - *To move boat by pushing the pole.*

Aegre - *Bore or tidal wave.*

Quarrage - *Small changes in tide on uppermost parts of the Severn.*

Freshet - *Faster flow of water due to rain.*

Dannell - *Word for water in Thames Valley.*

Fend off - *To push boat away to stop a collision with another boat or obstacle.*

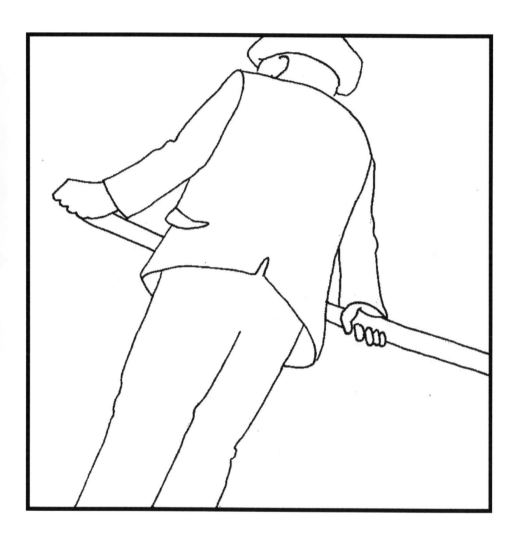

Legging - *To move a boat through a tunnel by lying on wooden planks and moving the boat by walking along the walls.*

Wings - *Flat boards used to lie on when legging. Two different sizes, short and long for legging in different width tunnels.*

Some canals were cut through hillsides and built without towpaths to save money, so the only way to move the boats was by Legging. Two 'leggers' would lie either side on wooden boards and literally walk their way through the canal. There were many accidents so boards called 'wings' were hooked onto either side of the bow to make it a bit safer. The longer tunnels such as Blisworth and Dudley employed professional leggers wearing brass arm bands to identify themselves.

Slack - *Small lumps of coal.*

Tunnel hook - *Hook on the stern of a butty, used for attaching ropes, helping to pull it through a tunnel.*

Sister Mary Ward

Sister Mary Ward was born in 1885 and was the daughter of Thomas Amos a twine and rope maker in a cottage on the edge of the canal at Stoke Bruerne. Later her husband Charlie Ward took over the business while she took care of her father. She gave her time and knowledge freely to the boat people, and local villagers, helping with their healthcare. In the 1930's she was recognised by the Grand union Canal Company and was employed as 'Consultant Sister to long distance boatmen and families'. In 1951 she received The British Empire Medal and continued working until 1962 when she retired. She was known to the boaters as
'The angel of the waterways'.

Fore - *Front of boat.*

Aft - *Back of boat.*

George Smith - *Campaigned in the 1870's and 1880's for better living conditions.*

A train of 'Tom Puddings'.
Tub boats were used from 1860 to 1985 to transport coal from the open cast south Yorkshire collieries near Stanley Ferry on the Aire and Calder Navigation to the port of Goole. Each tug could carry between 10 to 15 tons, but after the First World War the locks were enlarged so trains of 19 , each carrying 35 to 40 tons of coal, could work with a leader and tug .
The name could be after black puddings or Yorkshire puddings.

Jebus - *A bows-only section of a barge that was pushed between tub train and tug. This helped the handling.*

Plies - *To go to and fro.*

Boats bottom - *Empty hold.*

Wobble / 'To get a wobble on ' - *Moving quickly.*

Hobbling - *Running ahead to get locks ready.*

Hobbler - *Man or woman who gets the locks ready.*

Hobble - *Lock wheel.*

Lock Wheeler - *Person on a bicycle going ahead to open locks.*

Staunch, Flash lock, Navigation weir - *Weir with single gate.*

Back set /Turning a lock around - *Closing gates and resetting a lock once you have been through it for the benefit of the following boat.*

Balance pole / beam - *Used to push against to open gates. Balance Beams - Long beams that you push against to open and close the gates of a lock. The beam tapers and fixes into a mitre post.*

Barrel vaulted cottage on the Stratford canal.
Built for the ' lengthsman' who maintained the lock and the length of canal next to the lock. One of a series of six lock keepers' cottages built around 1812 as cheaply as possible by builders using bridge techniques, due to lack of money because of the Napoleonic Wars.

Lengthman - *Employee of a canal company in charge of a section of canal.*

Outside - *Side away from the towpath.*

Pound - *Stretch of water between locks.*

Benjo - *A sailor's term meaning a noisy day on the streets, onshore.*

The Board - *BWB British Waterways Board.*

Toll houses - *Octagonal shaped houses along the Birmingham Canals.*

Ganzie - *Sweater*

Hold in - *Steer boats towards towing path.*

Hold out - *Steer boats away from towing path.*

Chimley / Chimbley - *Chimney, black with brass bands and always on the left hand side.*

Chimley tin - *Open ended tins on top of cabin chimneys to improve the draught. Dried milk cans were popular.*

Well deck - *Where you stand to steer on a horse drawn boat.*

Counter deck - *Where you stand on modern boats. They are flat and are called counters.*

Counter - *Part of stern below the water.*

Tied up - *Moored.*

Packet boat - *Boat used for passengers, luggage and parcels.*

Tug - *Boat with no carrying space that tows another boat. An electric boat was used on the Harecastle Tunnel on the Trent and Mersey Canal. It was originally powered by batteries carried in a boat behind.*

B.C.N - *The Birmingham Canal Navigations.*

GUCCC - *Grand Union Canal Carrying Company.*

Dustbin or blue top - *Commercial narrowboats built in 1950's for British Transport Commission.*

Navigation lights - *White -front and back, Green right side, red left side.*

Composite craft - *Non powered vessels towed or attached to one powered vessel.*

Gunwale / 'gunals' - *Top edge of hull where it joins the cabin side, wide enough to walk along.*

Cants - *Rails or strips that edge the counter and foredeck of traditional narrowboat.*

Taff rail - *Guard rail around the counter.*

Uxterplate - *Steel bottom plate of counter deck, where it goes over the propeller and rudder.*

Narrow beam Tugs - *These tugs moved loaded lighters and were easy to 'wind' being narrow.*

Ring - *Taking a circular route, The Coventry Ring.*

Transom - *Cross beam or vertical bulkhead to strengthen stern.*

Ranters / Flashers - *Gate paddles on the bottom gates of lock.*

The boatmen wore corduroy suits and small checked cloth suits, each with matching waistcoats. Some cloth waistcoats had a key lock pattern cut out at the top, but all were cut straight across the bottom. Points were only seen after 1900. Instead of collars they wore big neckerchiefs, sometime just wrapped in front of the neck with the ends tucked under the shoulders of the waistcoat, and tied to their braces. Any ties and ribbons needed to be kept out of the way due to not wanting to be caught up in moving machinery such as locks.

Spider web embroidery - *Fancy stitching on men's belts.*

Moleskin - *Thick woollen cloth with a short pile.*

Bend - *Waistcoat.*

Billy - *Handkerchief.*

Dobbin - *Ribbon.*

Dunnage - *Clothes.*

Anderton boat lift - *Designed by Edwin Clarke. Lifted cargo boats 50 feet from the River Weaver to the Trent & Mersey Canal.*

Black boats - *Thomas Clayton short distance boats for carrying liquid in bulk.*

Brightwork - *Traditional paintwork on Leeds and Liverpool canal boats.*

Woolwich - *Large and small steel working boats built in London by Harland & Woolf.*

Ricky - *Boats built by Walker Brothers of Rickmansworth and nickname for the same town on the Grand Union.*

Barge - *A boat with a beam of over 12ft.*

Narrow canal boat - *Beam measuring less than 7ft 6".*

Wharf/ 'ampton boats - *Wolverhampton boats, 87ft long with a 7ft 9" beam. Often towed in trains by tugs on lock free canals.*

Star Class - *Boats named after constellations working for Grand Union C.C.C.*

Town Class - *Grand Union C.C.C. boats named after towns.*

Royalty Class boats - *1930's GUCC boats built to work on the widening and modernisation of the cut between London and Birmingham.*

River class boats/Blue tops - *Tanker narrowboats built for BWB. Owned by Thomas Clayton of Oldbury, all named after rivers.*

Admiral Class - *Built by Yarwoods of Northwich for BWB.*

Runcorn narrowboat - *Built six planks deep instead of five with a lower cabin. The canals are deeper around Manchester so the boats could carry more.*

The Packet House at Worsley

Passengers wishing to travel on the Bridgewater Canal, could buy their tickets from the Packet House. The bridge over the canal is known as the Alphabet bridge due to scholars practising their alphabet as they walked across the 26 planks.

Bridge hole - *Opening beneath bridge*
Junction - where two or more canals meet.

Stem - *Curved front end of boat.*

'Stemmed the bridge' - *Head on collision.*

Windward - *Facing the wind.*

Leeward - *Downwind, side sheltered from the wind.*

Voussoirs - *Stones that are cut to make an arch.*

Keystone - *Centre stone of arch.*

Staith - *A wharf used for loading coal.*

Basins - *Wide areas on waterways originally used for loading and unloading.*

Butty/ganger - *A man employed by the contractor to enlist a band of men to do certain works on the canal.*

Navvies - *Navigators.*

Loodel - *A staff used to extend the height of tiller when loaded with high loads.*

Stoppage - *The closing of a length of canal for maintenance.*

Hythe - *Wharf.*

Wayleave - *Part of a right of way that is rented.*

Navigationalists - *Itinerant labourers who built the canals.*

Cabin crochet
Used to decorate the edges of shelves, curtains, bonnets, shawls and pinnies. The lengths of lace had one straight edge and the other of 'vandyke points' also known as 'the pointed Rover'. The white cotton ' poor man's lace' could easily be boiled clean.

Ticket drawer piece - *Crochet edging.*

Ticket drawer - *Small drawer inside cabin, on left of door near ceiling. Jokingly said to be another place to sleep.*

Slide - *Sliding hatch on rear roof of boat.*

IW - *Idle women', nickname for the women working on the canals during WWII, from the initials on the badges that they wore.*

Cruiser - *Wooden or fibreglass pleasure boats.*

Dolly - *Fitting on counter to secure ropes.*

Tunnel cutter – *Semi-circular brass ring above the exhaust pipe on old boats.*

Pigeon box -*Ventilator above engine room*

Splitter, Cutter or Titch - *Small engine exhaust pipe with a loop of brass.*

Biscuit tin - *Also known as pigeon box, but square and often found on Joshers.*

Dog box - *A vent or skylight on narrowboat.*

Scumbling / scrumbling - *Painting using a coloured glaze to make fittings look like wood. Not only decorative and protective but disguised poor timber. Wood graining to look like Oak was a favourite. The same style was also used to decorate engines, train carriages, Gypsy wagons and the doors in houses.*

Combing - *Combing tools used in wood graining.*

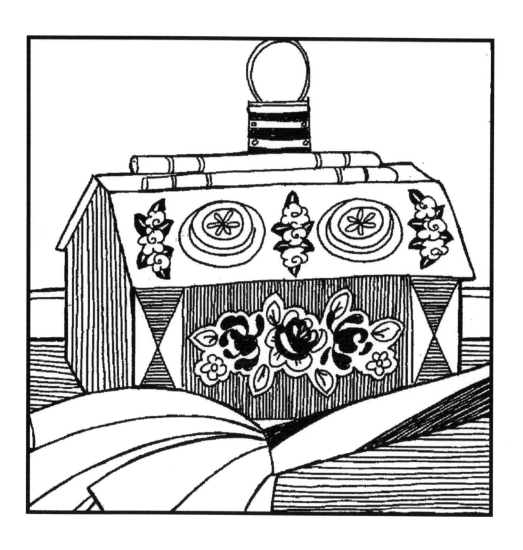

Crochet ear protectors for the working horses, decorated with tassels to keep flies away from their eyes.

Flash - *Looking smart.*

Collar - *Leather hoop, padded with straw around horses neck. Used for the horse to pull against and to distribute the weight.*

Hames - *Metal or wooden curved lengths used to connect collar to harness.*

Traces - *Straps or chains from hames on neck collar.*

Bit - *Piece of metal held in the horses mouth by the bridle, used for control.*

Crupper - *A soft leather loop that fits under the horses tail to stop the harness from slipping forward.*

Britchin' / Breeching strap - *Leather strap around haunches to allow horse to slow the towing vehicle down.*

Running blocks - *Half round wooden blocks with a hole in the middle, used to guide a rope from the mast to a stud on the cabin roof of a butty.*

Merchandise
Hogheads of cider.
Kilderkins of porter.
Cases of copper.
Firkins of lead.
Punny's of hemp.

Girder - *Thin rope used to tie down the top planks to the cross beam.*

Laden - *Loaded.*

Top planks/ Gang planks - *Planks held up by mast and stands along length of boat.*

Uprights - *Detachable planks from gunwales to top planks on working boats.*

Topsides - *Surface of hull above the waterline.*

Big - *Name of lock at Middlewich.*

Rumps - *Locks on the Trent and Mersey.*

Hell Meadow - *Name of locks at Wigan.*

Summit - *Highest point along canal or flight of locks.*

Turf locks - *Turf lined sloping sided locks.*

Bull nose/ Knuckle - *Rounded stonework at entrance to a lock.*

Stop gates - *Wooden gates that are kept open but can be shut to dam a canal, when it needs repairing.*

Stop grooves - *Where stop planks can be fitted, in narrow parts of a canal, often near locks.*

Stop planks - *Planks that fit into stop grooves, sometimes seen in piles near locks.*

Stank - *Temporary dam.*

Cratch - *Triangular board at bow of boat, originally where the horse feed was kept.*

Gongoozler- *People who watch rather than participate in all aspects of canal life. Sometimes used to refer to people being idle on the towpath.*

Cheesing - *Winding the ropes into a flat decorative spiral shape.*

Packet boat - *Boat used for passengers, luggage and parcels.*

Rubbing Strakes - *Raised wooden bands capped in metal, on ends of boats to help protect the hull from bumps and scrapes.*

Bulkheads - *Walls creating compartments.*

Gauging - *Boats sometimes paid a toll to Canal Companies depending on the weight they carried. This was gauged by how deep the boat was in the water.*

Titania

The 'Titania' was a butty built in Birmingham in 1922 working for Fellows, Morton and Clayton. It was paired with 'Little Woolwich" boat Themis starting work for the Grand Union Canal Carrying Company in 1935.

Titania - *Queen of the fairies in William Shakespeare's play A Midsummer night's dream.*

Dipper - *Metal bowl with handle.*

Rams head - *Wooden rudder post on a butty.*

Tingles - *Lengths of wood fixed horizontally onto Elum to strengthen it.*

Back door - *The door into cabin from the boats hold.*

Nip - *Narrow place along canal.*

Bell oil - *Hitting something hard.*

Oil rod - *The Bolinder engines speed control.*

Rods - *Engine controls on Bolinder Engines.*

Bolinder - *The diesel engine originally fitted into Fellows, Morton and Clayton boats.*

Bracket open - *High speed in a motor boat.*

Pup - *9hp Bolinder engine*

'Hot bulb' - *Semi diesel engine.*

Stuffing box - *Stern gland in engine.*

Morse - *A lever/gear for throttle control.*

Remote Greaser - *Metal cylinder filled with grease next to stern tube.*

Sea cock and mud box - *Canal or river water goes through hull into pipes to provide engine coolant.*

Boatwomens 'traditional' bonnet.
Fancy bonnets with strings tied behind the head and long at the back for sun protection.. Plain and patterned fabrics decorated with crochet lace and coloured piping. They were worn from the 1880's right through to and during the First World War. In 1901 many ladies wore black bonnets mourning the death of Queen Victoria.

Goffered - *Ornamental frill, made by pressing and pleating fabric.*

Kitcrew buggit - *Ghost in tunnel between Tunstall and Kitcrew.*

Spring heeled jack- Victorian urban legend of a frightening figure, ten foot high, who could make huge leaps and attacked people. Thought to have accompanied boats under a bridge on the Grand Union, west of London.

Flag/ pinner - *Apron.*

Luggers - *Earings.*

Measham Ware
The pottery was first made by William Mason at Church Gresley around 1870. It was sold by Mrs Annie Bonas in her shop at 'Cut End' Measham, adjacent to the Ashby canal in Leicestershire.
It is also known as 'Rockingham ware' and 'Bargeware'. They were particularly popular on the Midland and Oxford canals.

Tommy shop/ Tommy rot- *Employers would pay in copper tokens that were only exchangeable in the shop or public...often owned by the employer. Sometimes the food in the shop was so bad that it would give you 'Tommy rot'.*

Truck store - *Same as Tommy shop.*

Trucked - *Bartering or bartered.*

Pincher laddies / kiddies - *Old time Irish Navvies.*

Nipper - *Boys who worked for the navvies*

Flat - *A shallow punt used by lock keepers for maintenance on canal.*

Black flat - *Larger boat trading between the River Weaver and Liverpool.*

Iron day boat or Joey boat - *These boats from the Midlands, were often double ended, so the rudder could be fixed at either end saving time not having to turn around, and were generally used for short distances. The Birmingham day boats had no accommodation but the Joey boats often had cabins. They were pulled by horses and later with the development of diesel engines, a tug could pull a few at a time.*

Hopper - *Barge used for transporting dredged soil and rubbish.*

Railway / Station boats - *Day boats owned by railways around Birmingham, used for transferring goods from factories to sidings.*

Cock / Coggy boat - *Dinghy.*

Roses and Castles - *Name for decorative painting. A boat painter would flat paint, wood grain and do the sign writing as well.*

Cabbages - *Badly painted roses.*

Fettle - *Tidy up paintwork.*

Braunston -Frank Nurser and Ron Hough

Polesworth style – Henry (Harry) Atkins *and family.*
Edward Crowshaw *and his son* George.
Len Shakespeare.

Knob sticks - *Nickname for the Anderton Company. The boats carried a lot for the Staffordshire potteries.*

Knob stick roses - *More realistic style of painted roses first painted by* Bill Hodgson. Reg Barnett.

Tooley - George Tooley *of Tooley boatyard in Banbury, and his sons* George and Herbert.
Frank Jones - *GUCC and Fellows, Morton & Clayton*
George Baxter - *Barlow's.*
(Apologies to anyone I missed)

Wooser - *Nickname for narrowboat in the South Midlands.*

Reso's - *Residential boats built at ash vale on the Basingstoke canal.*

Oddn's - *Boats without accommodation.*

' Braunston rubbing rags' - *Boats working from London to Braunston.*

Greasy Wheelers - *Through boats.*

Mud heelers - *Boaters working on northern part of Oxford canal to Coventry.*

'Woolly backed 'uns ' - *Boats working London to Leicester.*

Barlow boat - *Coal boats around Birmingham.*

Shroppie Fly – *A fast 6ft wide boat used on the Shropshire Union and towed by two horses.*

Aqueducts - *Bridges carrying water over valleys, railway lines, roads and rivers. Locks were not needed because they kept the water level.*
Pontcysyllte - *1805 Thomas Telford aqueduct near Wrexham in Wales.*

Giggetty, Bumblehole, Dimmingsdale - *Bridge names on the Staffs and Worcs Canal.*

Accommodation bridge - *A bridge built for farmers when canals were built across their land.*

Inclined Plane- *A way of raising or lowering boats up and down a slope, instead of building locks. The boats are carried in either caisson tanks, cradles or slings, and use a type of railway.*
Caisson tank- *Water filled tank.*

The Hay - *Inclined plane at Iron Bridge Gorge, Shropshire.*

Trench – *Once the site of an inclined plane on Shropshire Canal near Telford.*

Washer Josher - *New boat trying to look old.*

Smarties - *False rivets.*

Noddy boat - *Any canal boat which isn't 70ft in length.*

GRP - *Glass reinforced plastic.*

Bobby dazzler - *A small light on top of rear of cabin or stern of motor.*

Single out - *To work boats in tandem*

Wherry - *A rowing boat used to carry passengers.*

'Mind the grease' - *Can you let me pass by.*

Good Road - *All the locks are ready to use straight away.*

Bad road – *The opposite, every lock needing emptying or filling.*

Roving / turnover bridge - *A bridge carrying the towpath from one side of the canal to the other. Horses could walk up and over the bridge to change towpaths without un-hitching from butty.*

To blow - *To warn other boats of your presence, especially near to a bridge'ole or narrow place with no view ahead.*

Blow-up Bridge - *Macclesfield Bridge which was blown up accidentally by a boat carrying gunpowder.*

Banbury stick - *A pole used for propping up lift bridges.*

Bull nose/ Knuckle - *Rounded stonework at entrance to a lock.*

Side Bridge - *Bridge taking towpath over a canal branch.*

The 'Buckby' can

The generic term for the painted water cans. LTC Rolt bought a can from Top Lock Cottage, long Buckby, Northamptonshire and mentioned it in his book 'Narrowboat'. Since then they have been known as Buckby cans. At the time they were lots of different styles, some called Cheshire, Braunston and knobstick cans. They were painted with roses and castles
They were used to carry clean water and were owned by individual boatmen rather than the canal companies.

Tumblehome - *The sloping sides of the stern cabin.*

Back door - *Door in forend of cabin.*

Clinker built - *Wooden boats with overlapping planks.*

Knot - *Speed measurement.*

Bed'ole - *Bed cupboard. A door / seat behind the curtains, pulls down to create a small double bed. (Cross bed).*

Berth - *Sleeping quarters on boats.*

Ribbon plates - *Decorative plates with pierced edging, often threaded with ribbons.*

To stove - *To get rid of bugs by fumigating with sulphur.*

Sprat - *Sixpence.*

Teviss / Hog / Gen - *Shilling.*

Glistener / Thick'un /Jane / Jemmy- *Sovereign.*

Ray - *One and sixpence.*

Joey -*Fourpence piece.*

Jack - *Farthing.*

Flatch - *Half penny.*

Dry dock - *Usually a basin that can be flooded to bring boat in then drained. The boat can then be easily worked on.*

Brindley's spoon - *A tool for emptying water from the canal. As it was lowered into the water a leather flap opened, then closed as it was lifted out.*

Bat - *One of the blades of a boat propeller.*

Lay - *A wider section of the basin where a boat could moor away from channel.*

Tunnel bands - *Coloured bands on back of narrowboats, often cream and red.*

Mast - *A square wooden post with steel topmast and luby, used for bow hauling and for towing a butty.*

Mast Beam - *The cross beam that the mast fits into.*

Middle beam - *The beam next to mast beam Having the stand fitted into it.*

Mitre gate -*The mitre gate is credited as being designed by Leonardo da Vinci (1452 - 1519). Two gates mitred at the edge where they meet.*

Pound lock - *The pound lock is said to have been invented by Chhiao Wei-Yo in 983 China. Two sets of gates with a pound between.*

Side ponds - *Used to keep plenty of water available on locks. It could be filled when emptying a lock so then used to help fill.*

Sills / Cills - *A solid shelf of stone or concrete at the top end of every lock. Under water when lock is full and used to hold the top gates against the weight of the water from the pound above.*

Breasting up - *Two boats working or travelling, tied side by side.*

Cloughs - *Gate or ground paddles.*

Muddling - *Dredging canals and watercourses by hand.*

Puddle - *Clay used to make the bottom and sides of a canal watertight.*

Slub/ slutch - *Mud from dredging.*

Suff - *Ditch or drain.*

Ballasting - *Dredging using a scoop.*

Longboat - *Name used for a narrowboat on the River Severn.*

Long dog - *Lurcher, greyhound or whippet.*

Anser/answer pins - *Hooks and shackles at stern of boat. Used for breasting up or for strapping.*

Crumb - *Slabs of milk, cocoa and sugar that were transported by boat for the Cadbury Factory in Birmingham.*

Snatch - *A tow.*

Agen - *Against.*

Shoots/ Shutts - *The false floors in the hold of a narrowboat.*

Wooser - *A word used in the South Midlands to describe a narrow boat.*

Amidship - *Middle of boat.*

Boat snapper - *Man who moves unattended boats during unloading or loading.*

Stroving - *To be working hard.*

Tunnel lamp - *Lamp fixed on cratch for navigating in the dark.*

Bow - *Forend.*

Bow thruster - *Small propeller on Bow section.*

Strapping in - *Stopping the boat by using a rope around a post.*

Strapping stump - *Bollard.*

Dolly - *Round mooring bollard.*

Bowhauling - *To tow a boat by hand without the help of a horse.*

Penstock - *Conduit pipe with a valve for emptying a canal quickly.*

Toe - *Bottom of an embankment,*

Head gate - *Top or upper gates of lock that let water in.*

Tail gate - *Gates that let water out, lower gates.*

Heel / Coin post - *The post on which the lock gates hang.*

Crop beams - *Nine horizontal parts of lock gate.*

Horse marines - *Yorkshire contractors who use horses for haulage.*

Animal / Hanimal - *Donkeys or mules used for towing, instead of horses.*

Backering - *A horse that can be left to tow a boat without being led.*

Hold back - *When horses pulling boats could be stopped in an emergency.*

Bobbins - *Hollow wooden rollers fixed to traces to prevent rubbing. They were often brightly painted in primary colours.*

Looby Luby - *An attachment for towing ropes for butties and horses drawn boats near the bow.*

Tackle - *Horse harness.*

Hostler / ostler - *A man employed to look after the horses in riverside pubs and hotels.*

Gail - *A horse.*

Greasy ockers -
Boaters who worked Fellows, Morton and Clayton boats.

Fellows, Morton and Clayton.
The company was founded in 1837 by James Fellows in West Bromwich. In 1876 his son Joshua was joined by Frederick Morton. Thomas Clayton joined in 1889. In 1947 the 'British Transport Commission' took the company over.

Josher - *Boats used by Fellows, Morton and Clayton.*

Monkey boat - *A nickname for traditional narrowboats that worked on the Grand Union Canal and London waterways. Might be named after Thomas Monk who designed the first living cabin on the boats he owned in London.*

Severn Trow - *Old sailing boats once used on the Severn Estuary.*

Oakum - *Shredded rope and pitch used to seal between planks.*

Trenail – *Oak pegs used for joining wood in wooden boats and barges.*

Chalico/ tat - *Hot horse and cow dung used for dressing timber on wooden boats.*

Blacking - *Applying black bitumen to steel hulls.*

Caulking - *Hammering in oakum between timber joints on boats.*

Rampers - *Spikes driven between planks to hold them together on wooden boats.*

Graving - *The cleaning and repainting of boats hulls.*

Watercress bed - *Leaking boat.*

Rodney boat – *An old badly maintained or scruffy boat.*

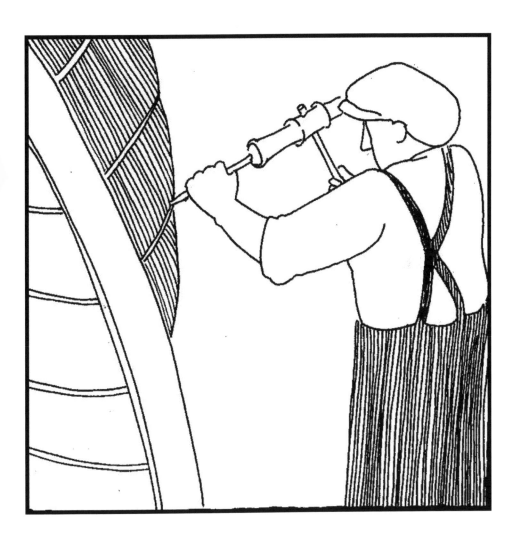

Side-bed - *The long locker seat inside the cabin on the starboard side.*

Table-cupboard - *A rounded top cupboard door, hinged at its base that pulls down to sit on a strong shelf and becomes a table top.*

Blacking/Monkey box - *A small sloping lidded box in alcove on the right under a cupboard.*

Crumb drawer - *Knife drawer below table cupboard door.*

Bright bits - *Decorative brass bits and bobs.*

Soap 'ole - *Two shelves next to ticket Drawer.*

Rasher wagon - *Frying pan*

Scran – *Food*

Starvationers – *Narrow Worsley boats working in the underground collieries, owned by The Duke of Bridgewater.*

Printed in Great Britain
by Amazon